The Ant and the Grasshopper

An Aesop's Fable

Retold by Jenny Giles
Illustrated by Pat Reynolds

Once upon a time,
a little ant lived in a beautiful meadow.

All summer long, the grass grew tall,
and the flowers were bright and colorful.

The ant had made an underground home
for her family in the meadow.
She worked hard and was always busy.

2

Nearby, there lived a grasshopper. He sang and danced all day long. There was plenty of food to eat, and life was good in the meadow. He hadn't a care in the world.

3

But soon the cooler days of autumn arrived.

The ant knew that it was time
to prepare for the coming winter.
So she spent many hours
gathering seeds, and carrying them
back to her home.

4

But the grasshopper just sat in the sun.
Sometimes he watched the busy little ant
running backward and forward
through the long grass.

"Why do you bother to work so hard?"
asked the grasshopper.
"It is much more fun to sing and dance."

And he jumped about in the long grass,
chirping happily to himself.

The ant said to the grasshopper,
"You are a very foolish creature
if you do not know
that winter will soon be here.
When the snow comes,
there will be no food to be found.
Then you will starve."

But the grasshopper paid no attention to the wise little ant.

"You are just wasting your time!" he laughed.
"We have more than enough to eat! And besides, why should I gather food that I might not need?"

And he danced away through the meadow, singing his favorite song.

All too soon,
the days began to grow colder.
It became much harder to find food.

One morning,
the ant and the grasshopper awoke
to find the meadow covered in snow.

The ant was able to shelter
down in her home.
But the grasshopper had to jump about
on the frozen ground.

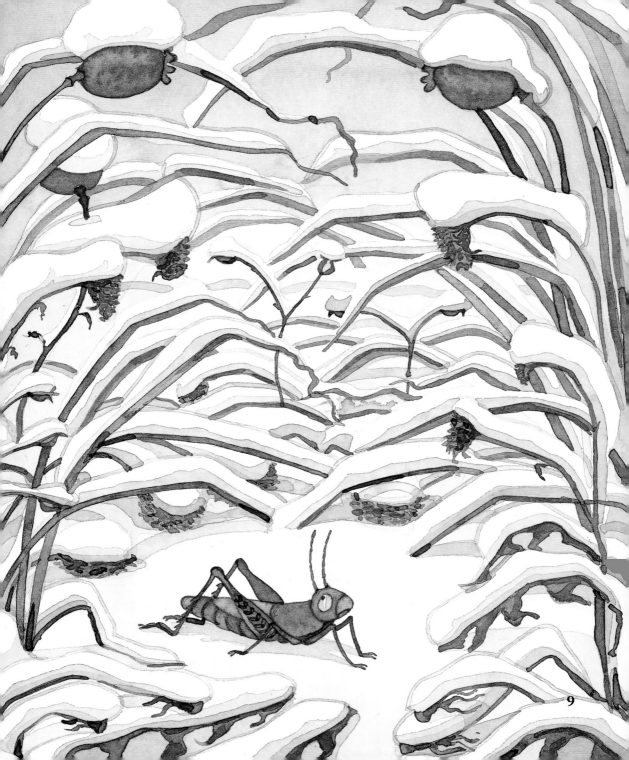

In the days that followed,
snow kept falling.
A cold wind blew across the meadow.

The ant and her family
stayed safe and warm.
Every day, they ate some of the seeds
that they had gathered during the autumn.

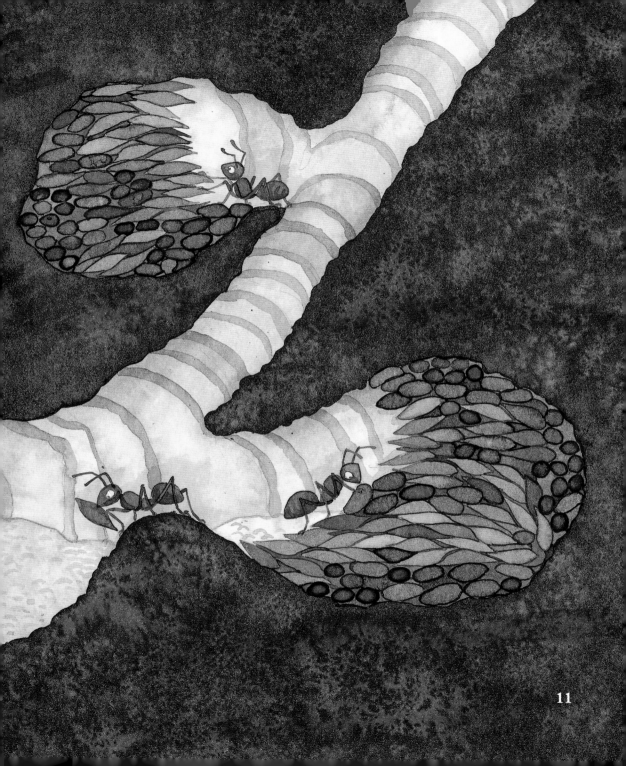

But the grasshopper was finding
that the meadow in winter
was a very different place.
Now he had to spend his days
looking for something to eat.

After a few weeks,
he became very thin and miserable.
He went to see the ant
in her underground home.

"I'm freezing out here in the meadow,"
he cried. "And I'm starving, too!
Please let me have some of your food!"

The ant looked out at the grasshopper.
"I worked for many hours
to gather this food in the autumn,"
she said.
"And you paid no attention when I said
that winter was on the way.
Besides, there are only a few seeds left.
I'm sorry, but I have just enough
to feed my family!"

Then the ant said to the grasshopper,
"However, you are lucky.
Winter is almost over,
and spring is coming.
Very soon, there will be plenty of food
in the meadow for all of us."

The grasshopper crawled away,
knowing how foolish he had been.
And by the time the snow had disappeared,
he was a much wiser creature indeed.